EARLY THEMES

5 Senses

Ready-to-Go Activities, Games, Literature Selections, Poetry, and Everything You Need for a Complete Theme Unit

by Tracey West

SCHOLASTIC
PROFESSIONAL BOOKS

NEW YORK • TORONTO • LONDON • AUCKLAND • SYDNEY

Edited by Joan Novelli
Cover design by Vincent Ceci and Jaime Lucero
Cover illustration by Jo Lynn Alcorn
Interior design by Solutions by Design, Inc.
Interior illustration by Abby Carter

ISBN 0-590-13112-5

12 11 10 9 8 7   01/0

Contents

About this Book

As a teacher of young children, it's no surprise that teaching the five senses—sight, hearing, taste, smell, and touch—is a key part of your school year. That's probably because so much of the curriculum for early learners centers on the world around your students—their relationships with friends and family, their neighborhood, their bodies, and their feelings. An understanding of the five senses helps students make important connections as they explore their world.

This book is designed to help you teach and celebrate the five senses with your students. You'll find:

◎ Senses at Work, an interactive poster

◎ ideas and instructions for creating a Five Senses Learning Center and keeping it going;

◎ activities for launching your unit;

◎ appealing cross-curricular lessons for exploring each of the five senses, including activities, experiments, extensions, and literature connections;

◎ science background on each of the five senses that you can use for your own information or adapt to share with students;

◎ age-appropriate reproducibles, including a mini-book;

◎ suggestions for wrapping up the unit and celebrating students' discoveries.

You can use the ideas, activities, and materials as they appear or customize them to create your own Five Senses theme unit.

TEACHING WITH THEMES

Teachers who use themes find they serve as a convenient framework for structuring lessons, and especially for integrating curriculum areas in meaningful ways. Children benefit from theme units, too, which allow them to revisit concepts over time, deepening their understanding. So, for example, while students experiment with their sense of touch, they'll also explore adjectives that descibe how things feel, create graphs about fingerprint patterns, and write their own touchable books—each activity reinforcing concepts in different ways and strengthening students' understandings.

GETTING READY

Materials

To begin, you'll want to make a list of materials you'll need, and take inventory to see which ones you have on hand. (Many of the activities use materials you may already have.) You may wish to write a letter to parents, sharing information about the theme and listing materials they might donate.

Grouping

Many of the lessons invite students to work in small, cooperative groups. Groups come in handy if you decide to create a learning center, too. (See page 5.) One way to handle this is to assign groups from the outset, for example, dividing the class into five groups, one for each sense. Children can then design symbols to represent their groups.

Assessment

Before beginning the theme, prepare a manila folder for each child. Children can write their names on their folders, and decorate with symbols and pictures related to the five senses. Have children use the folders throughout the theme to store the stories, poems, reproducibles, and other projects they complete. When you want to assess students' growth and progress, you'll have an easy and convenient source of information.

Note: *If you choose to display students' work in the classroom, remind students to place work they remove from displays in their folders.*

SETTING UP A LEARNING CENTER

While it isn't necessary to create a learning center in order to use the lessons in the book, a learning center can enhance learning in many ways. For example, learning centers:

◎ act as a visual focal point for a theme, and can encourage student interest and participation;

◎ allow all students to become involved in the theme, giving students opportunities to work in groups as well as independently;

◎ encourage students to assist one another in different ways, giving each child a chance to shine;

◎ provide a central location for storing theme materials and projects; and

◎ encourage children's independence in learning.

Here's one way to organize a learning center in your classroom. If you'd like to learn more, the book *Learning Centers: Getting Them Started, Keeping Them Going* by Michael F. Opitz (Scholastic, 1994) combines theory with practical suggestions.

Five Senses Learning Center

If you have limited classroom space, or if you already have other learning centers in operation in your classroom, then this option is for you. The Five Senses Learning Center is a simple center that will serve as a focal point for your theme.

To create any learning center, it helps to have a workspace, such as a table or desk, and wall space. A bookshelf, chairs, and floor mats are all useful additions. Suggestions for setting up a Five Senses Learning Center follow. Feel free to incorporate your own ideas, too.

◎ **DECORATE THE CENTER.** Use the wall space by the center to hang the Senses at Work poster, cut-out pictures of eyes, ears, noses, mouths, and hands, and any work that your students create during the theme, including pictures, posters, graphs, and word webs.

◎ **DISPLAY ASSORTED READING MATERIALS.** Collect books that relate to the five senses (see literature connections throughout this book). Add students' poems and books, and class books that you create. Children can visit the center to read books or share one another's work about the five senses.

◎ USE THE CENTER AS AN ACTIVITY HUB.

Plan a different activity at the center each day. Look for Learning Center Links throughout the book for suggestions. You may also find that particular activities lend themselves to a learning center setup. The Guessing Box (see page 36), Memory Magic (see page 10), and Taste Test (see page 26) are just three examples. Set out baskets or shoe boxes to hold supplies. Post written instructions if you like.

Scheduling Tip

To keep your learning centers running smoothly, post a daily or weekly schedule in a place where students can see it. You may fill in the schedule with students' names, or use cut-out symbols (eyes, ears, etc.) to represent each group.

The Five Senses Learning Center

Weekly Schedule

Monday

Tuesday

Wednesday

Thursday

Friday

Professional Resources

Instant Thematic Stationery for Beginning Writers coordinated by Liza Schafer (Scholastic Professional Books, 1995). This collection of reproducibles supports 30 different themes.

Learning Centers: Getting Them Started, Keeping Them Going by Michael F. Opitz (Scholastic, 1994). This practical guide includes management tips, scheduling ideas, suggested topics and activities, and reproducibles.

101 Science Poems and Songs for Young Learners (Scholastic, 1996). Easy, fun, fact-filled poems and songs that reinforce essential science concepts including the five senses and the human body.

Scholastic's The Magic School Bus Explores the Human Body (Microsoft, 1995). Join Ms. Frizzle in this interactive science adventure into Arnold's body (CD-ROM).

3-D Kids by Roger Culbertson and Robert Margulies (Freeman, 1995). This life-sized pop-up guide to the human body includes descriptions of how the body works (including eyes, ears, etc.), plus lots of fun facts.

The Ultimate Human Body (Dorling Kindersley Multimedia, 1994). This CD-ROM takes you on an interactive tour of the body.

Launching the Theme

What do your students know about their five senses? The following lesson introduces the topic and gives you an opportunity to assess students' prior knowledge of the subject. In addition to the lesson, you may wish to take students on a tour of the Five Senses Learning Center and review procedures (or work together to develop a list of center rules).

Subsequent sections explore each sense in depth, one at a time (except for taste and smell, which are closely linked and therefore taught together). They are not in any particular order; you can follow the order of the book, or flip through and choose one that you and your students find most appealing.

Our Five Senses

Students work together to make a class big book about the five senses.

Materials

◎ 6 sheets of chart paper or 11-by-17-inch construction paper

◎ crayons, paint, markers

Teaching the Lesson

1 Your students may already have some knowledge of the five senses and how they work. Begin by explaining that we have five senses that tell us about the world around us. Ask: Can anyone name any of these senses? Fill in gaps in students' knowledge by discussing one sense at a time. For example: Our sense of sight helps us to see the world around us. What part of our bodies do we see with?

2 Prepare the pages of the big book: On the first sheet of chart paper, write the title of the book, *Our Five Senses* (or a name students choose). On subsequent pages, write the following sentences for each sense, one set of sentences per page:

I see with my eyes.

I see _____.

3 Divide students into five groups, one for each sense: sight, hearing, touch, taste, and smell. Give each group its big book page. Read the text on the page aloud with each group. Children can then come up with a list of things they can see, hear, feel, taste, or smell, and draw those things on their page. Work with students to write the names of the items they've chosen on the page. For example, a finished page might read:

I see with my eyes.

I see my teacher, a tree, my friend Maria, and a hamster.

Note: *If you wish, you can suggest that children choose one item to complete the sentence.*

4 Let groups take turns decorating part of the big book cover (with eyes, noses, ears, mouths, hands, and so on). Bind pages with staples, paper fasteners, O-rings, or yarn loops. Then bring the class together and share the finished book.

 ACTIVITY Extension Play a quick game of How Many Senses? with students. Name an activity, and ask students to count how many senses they use when performing this activity. For example:

◎ lining up when the bell rings (hearing and sight);

◎ looking at a sunset (sight);

- playing catch with a friend (touch, sight, hearing);
- eating a piece of pizza (touch, taste, smell, sight).

 **Literature Connection** *My Five Senses* by Aliki (HarperCollins, 1989) is a wonderful introduction to this unit. After reading the book aloud, use questions to guide a discussion about senses, such as: What sense do you use when you look at the pictures in this book? What sense do you use when you eat a bowl of cereal?

Sight

From the colors in a paint box to a starry night sky, our eyes are our windows to the wonders of the world. In this section, children will explore how their sense of sight works day and night, and find out how their eyes can play tricks on them, too.

 **SCIENCE NOTES**

When eyes view an object, light reflects off of that object and enters the eye through the pupil. The lens focuses the images upside down and projects them onto light-sensitive cells on the retina (the membrane that lines the eye). These cells are called rods and cones. Rods detect black-and-white images and work well in dim light. Cones detect color images and do not work well in dim light.

When the rods and cones send an image to your brain, the brain turns the image right side up. The left eye and right eye see things from slightly different angles. The brain joins the two images to make a "3-D" picture.

Jungle Journey

Students use their imaginations to describe things they might see on a journey through the deep, dark jungle.

Teaching the Lesson

1 Arrange students in a circle on the floor in front of you. Tell students that they're about to go on an exciting journey. Instruct students to put on their "boots" and "helmets." It's time to take a walk through the jungle!

2 On a chalkboard or large flip chart, write the following rhyme:

I went to the jungle and what did I see?

I saw a _____ looking at me!

3 Read aloud the rhyme to students and ask them to help you fill in the blank with something they might see in the jungle. You might begin by giving students an example.

4 Have the class read the first line together, then invite students to take turns filling in the blank as they recite the second line. Repeat to give all students a turn. Add movement to the exercise by having students march in place through the jungle journey (optional).

ACTIVITY Extension Write the rhyme on a flip chart. Attach Velcro strips above the blank lines and to the back of word strips. Write the names of jungle animals and plants on half the strips, and the names of things that do not belong **in the** jungle on the other half (octopus, puppy, skyscraper, tractor, etc.). Ask students to choose words that would fit in the blanks.

Literature Connection Share *Brown Bear, Brown Bear, What Do You See?* by Eric Carle (Henry Holt, 1983). Ask students to identify similar sentence patterns in the book. Can they recognize the same pattern in the jungle rhyme?

 **Learning Center Link**

Write the rhyme on a chart or large piece of poster board. Attach a strip of Velcro above the blank line. Use construction paper or poster board and Velcro strips to make word strips with the words students used to fill in the blank. Let students retell the rhyme by attaching the word strips to the chart.

Memory Magic

Students experience firsthand an important function of sight—its role in helping us to memorize things.

Materials

For each pair of students:

- two sets of small objects (such as a crayon, a feather, a spool of thread, a marble, and so on)
- a small blanket or piece of cloth
- clock with second hand, or stopwatch
- paper and pencil

Teaching the Lesson

1. Introduce the concept of memory and memorization to students. Give students examples of some things they may have committed to memory: their names, their phone numbers, and so on. Invite students to share any strategies they have for memorizing things. Explain that one way we memorize things is by forming a picture in our head of what we are trying to remember.

2. Divide students into pairs. Assign roles to each student in a pair: Partner 1 and Partner 2. Instruct Partner 1 to lay out the objects on a desk or other flat surface.

3. While Partner 1 watches the clock, give Partner 2 one minute to memorize the objects. This might be a good time to share some simple memorization tips, such as voicing the objects aloud, or making a silent list of the objects and repeating the list over and over.

4. When the minute is up, have Partner 1 cover the objects with a cloth. Ask Partner 2 to name the objects, or record them on a sheet of paper using words or pictures. Partners can then check the guesses together.

5. Have students switch roles and repeat steps 3 and 4, using a fresh set of objects.

ACTIVITY Extension Older students may be able to use mnemonic devices to help them with memorization. For example, if the four objects were a ball, a marble, a crayon, and a seashell, students could use the first letter of each to make a sentence: Blue monkeys color silently. The sentence is easier to memorize than a list, and letter clues are reminders of the object.

Literature Connection These books require students to look closely at a variety of pictures and objects to find the answers to fun rhymes and riddles.

◎ *Each Peach Pear Plum* by Janet and Allan Ahlberg (Scholastic, 1985)

◎ The *I Spy* series, with riddles by Jean Marzollo and photographs by Walter Wick (Scholastic)

Learning Center Link

Set up a variation of the game for students to play in small groups at the center. Display assorted objects on a tray. Have one child remove an object and place it behind his or her back while the others close their eyes. When they open their eyes, can the children spot which item is missing?

SCIENCE/ART

Eyes Play Tricks

Our eyes love to play tricks on us! In this lesson, students experience optical illusions in action.

Materials

◎ optical illusion reproducible (see page 14)

◎ crayons

Teaching the Lesson

1. Ask students: Why do you think we have two eyes? Why do you think we don't have just one eye in the middle of our foreheads? These questions will help students start thinking about the way their two eyes see the world from different angles. The brain takes the images (or pictures) seen by each eye and combines them to make one image.

You can explain that sometimes our brains get confused by the images sent by our eyes. When this happens, our brain is tricked into seeing things that aren't real.

2. Give each student a copy of the optical illusion reproducible. Ask students to touch their noses to the page in between the flower and the bee while keeping their eyes open. What do they see? (The bee appears to fly into the flower.) Explain that their eyes have just played a trick on their brains!

3. Invite students to experiment with making their own optical illusions using the bottom part of the reproducible. Demonstrate how to draw two objects exactly two inches apart. Brainstorm combinations to try, such as an open mouth and a piece of cake, a swimming pool and a dolphin, a tunnel and a train, and so on. Have students test their optical illusions then share them with classmates.

SCIENCE

Colors in the Dark

Lights out! In this lesson, students learn how their eyes react to dim light.

Materials

For each small group:

◎ shoe box or other small box

◎ 3 pairs of dark-colored socks (each a different color)

◎ 1 pair of white or light-colored socks

Teaching the Lesson

1. Mix up each group's socks and place them in a box.

2. Ask students in each group to match the socks in their box.

3. Now explain that the task is going to get a little bit harder. Instruct students to mix up the socks and return them to the box. Then turn off the lights in the room, closing the shades if necessary. Ask students to try matching the socks in the box again.

4. When students are finished, turn on the lights. Ask: Was it easier or harder to sort the socks this time? Were you able to make matching pairs? Which pair was easiest to match? (The white pair.) Explain that the parts of our eyes that help us see colors, called *cones*, do not work well in the dark. When it's dark out, we're only able to see black, white, and shades of gray.

ACTIVITY Extension Remind students how much easier it was to match the white pair of socks than the other pairs. Based on this observation, what do students think would be a good color to wear if they wanted to be seen on a dark night? How can wearing light colors in the dark help keep people safe?

Literature Connection Share *Midnight Farm* by Reeve Lindbergh (Dial, 1987), a gentle story of a mother who guides a frightened child through the transition from day into night. Invite students to share their own feelings about the night.

My Shadow

Students practice math skills when they measure their own shadows.

Materials

For each pair of students:

◎ sidewalk chalk

◎ measuring tape

◎ flashlight (optional)

Teaching the Lesson

Note: *This activity needs to be performed outside on a sunny day. If you don't want to wait for a sunny day, you can work inside, having children shine flashlights behind one another (and assorted objects) onto a white wall or floor to cast shadows.*

1. Take students outside and challenge them to find as many shadows as they can. Can they find shadows cast by trees? Walls? Fences? Themselves?

2. Divide students into pairs. Have students in each pair take turns tracing each other's shadows on the ground with chalk.

3. Ask students to measure their shadows and write the results inside their shadows along with their names. Ask: Whose shadow is tallest? Whose shadow is most like your own?

4. Have students measure each other from head to toe. Are they taller or shorter than their shadows?

5. Direct students' attention to the shadows they spotted earlier. Invite them to estimate whether the other shadows are taller or shorter than their own, then use the measuring tape to test their guesses.

ACTIVITY Extension Use shadows to make silhouettes. Ask each "subject" to sit in a chair, whose side is facing the wall. Attach an 11-by-17-inch piece of dark construction paper to the wall, level with the subject's head. While one child shines a light on the subject, have another trace the outline of the subject's profile onto the paper. Children can cut out their silhouettes and write their names on the back with white chalk. Display silhouettes at the learning center. Can children guess whose silhouette is whose?

Literature Connection Soft watercolors illustrate an imaginative exploration of shadow play in *I Have a Friend* by Keiko Naharashi (McElderry, 1987). Multicultural art adds to the picture-book poem *My Shadow* by Robert Louis Stevenson (Putnam, 1990). Both make a rich addition to this lesson.

Learning Center Link

Let students perform a shadow-puppet play. Choose a familiar story such as Goldilocks and the Three Bears. *Have students begin by drawing and cutting out the story characters on cardboard. Help students add features by cutting details into the cardboard. Tape puppets to craft sticks or straws, as shown. Show students how to shine a light behind the puppets in a darkened room to cast shadows on the wall. Have students practice their show, then act out the tale as a narrator reads it.*

Eyes Play Tricks

Draw your own optical illusion.
Make your objects two inches apart.

Hearing

Hands clapping, school bells ringing, buses honking—your students' world is filled with sound each day. In this section, you'll find lessons for exploring familiar sounds, rhyme, and music. A special lesson on sign language introduces students to this rich form of silent communication.

SCIENCE NOTES

Sounds are vibrations. When sound vibrations reach the ear, they travel inside the ear canal to the eardrum. As the eardrum vibrates, nerves send messages to the brain, which interprets the sound.

City Sounds, Country Sounds

Students provide the sound effects for a "radio play" based on the folktale *The City Mouse and the Country Mouse*.

Materials

- a tape recorder
- a 60-minute cassette tape (30 minutes each side)
- a box of noisemaking items, such as bells, horns, whistles, and drumsticks (optional)

Teaching the Lesson

1 Have students heard the story of the country mouse and city mouse before? Spend some time discussing the two places featured in the story (the country and the city). Ask: Where do you live? In the country, in the city, or just outside one of these places? What do you already know about the country? About the city?

2 Read the play aloud. On the second read, invite students to use their voices and join in by making sound effects at appropriate moments (cows mooing, horns honking, etc.). You may wish to call on individual students for each sound effect.

3 Inform students that you'll be recording the play. Explain: Before television was invented, people gathered around the radio to listen to radio plays. Sound effects helped listeners imagine what was happening in the stories. When you record *The City Mouse and the Country Mouse*, you'll be doing the same thing.

4 Rehearse the play until students can perform the sound effects automatically. When students are ready, record the play.

5 Following the performances, ask: Why do you think the city noises bother the country mouse and not the city mouse? Why do you think the country noises bother the city mouse and not the country mouse? What kinds of noises do you hear at night? Create two columns on the chalkboard: *Country Sounds* and *City Sounds*. Invite students to classify the sound effects in the play in these two categories. (You may decide that some sounds belong in both!)

6 Try retelling the play, adding new city and country sound effects, such as a clock on a corner or a rooster on a fence.

ACTIVITY Extension Divide students into small groups and assign each group a sound effect. Have each group look through a box of various noisemaking items—bells, horns, and so on—and try to create the sound effects in the radio play with one or more of these tools.

Literature Connection Students will enjoy identifying sounds they know in the picture book *City Sounds* by Craig Brown (Greenwillow Books, 1992). Challenge them to add new sounds, too.

Learning Center Link

Copy the play on chart paper, leaving blank spaces for the words that describe sound effects. Write these words on cards, then glue Velcro to the back of each card and to the spaces on the chart paper. Let children try to complete the story by putting the words in place.

The City Mouse and the Country Mouse

Once upon a time a country mouse visited a city mouse. That night when the country mouse settled in for a good night's sleep, the sounds of the busy street kept her awake.

The cars on the street honked, "Beep! Beep!"

The buses on the street roared, "Vroom! Vroom!"

The jackhammers in the street sang, "Rat-a-tat-tat."

The police officer on the corner whistled, "Tweet! Tweet!"

The fire engine called, "Whoo! Whoo!"

The country mouse didn't sleep a wink.

"I'm sorry, cousin," said the country mouse the next morning. "Your city street is much too noisy. Why don't you come to the country with me? It's quiet there."

"I don't think the city is noisy at all," said the city mouse. "But I will come to the country with you just the same."

So the city mouse and country mouse went to the country mouse's home. That night, when the city mouse settled in for a good night's sleep, the sounds of the country kept her awake.

The cows in the field bellowed, "Moo! Moo!"

The frogs in the creek croaked, "Ribbit! Ribbit!"

The crickets in the grass sang, "Chirp! Chirp!"

The chicks in the henhouse said, "Peep! Peep! Peep!"

The horse in the barn called, "Neigh! Neigh!"

The city mouse didn't sleep a wink.

"I'm sorry, cousin," said the city mouse the next morning. "Your country home is much too noisy for me. I think I'll go back to the city."

And so the city mouse returned to the city, and the country mouse stayed in the country, and that night they both got a good night's sleep.

Rhyme Time

This lesson uses the sense of hearing as a springboard for exploring an important language tool—rhyme!

Materials

- ◎ chart paper
- ◎ marker
- ◎ construction paper (optional)
- ◎ glue (optional)
- ◎ Velcro strips (optional)

Teaching the Lesson

1 Begin by introducing (or reviewing) the concept of rhyme with students. Write the following pairs of words on the board: see/bee, ear/hear, nose/rose, feel/peel, taste/paste. Read the words aloud. Ask: What do these pairs of words have in common? Students might recognize that these words sound alike, or rhyme. (Some students may notice that the words contain similar letter groups. If so, you may wish to expand the lesson by discussing selected letter groups and the sounds they indicate.)

2 Copy the nonsense poem "On the Ning Nang Nong" by Spike Milligan onto chart paper. (See page 19.) Leave a blank space in place of the last word in lines 2 (Bong), 5 (Ping), 6 (Joo), 8 (Clang), 9 (do), 11 (Bong), 13 (Ping), 15 (Clang), and 17 (Nong).

3 Now it's rhyme time! Read the poem aloud. Invite students to fill in the blank spaces with words that fit the rhyme scheme of the poem. Because this is a nonsense poem, anything goes! Made-up rhyming words will work just as well as familiar words. Write students' choices in the blank spaces.

4 Divide the class into three groups: cows, trees, and mice. As you read the final version of your poem aloud, have each group chime in with its rhyming word.

5 Wrap up the lesson by asking: Can you think of any other poems, songs, or verses that rhyme? Students may be surprised to realize how many rhymes they already know. Write some familiar rhyming verses (such as "Humpty Dumpty" or "Mary Had a Little Lamb") on chart paper, leaving some of the rhyming words out. Challenge children to fill in the missing words.

ACTIVITY Extension Keep your students' rhyme skills sharp by holding a Rhyming Bee. Divide the class into two teams. Have each team take turns coming up with a rhyme for a word you choose from a Rhyme Time List. (Students who are able can write their answers on the chalkboard.) The whole class wins when there's a rhyme for each of the words on your list. You can use these words for your Rhyme Time List, or come up with your own: say, see, eye, row, blue, bat, feet, boat, sing, dog, face, lean, ball, rice, sun, rain, cold, four, ate, sand.

Literature Connection "A told B, and B told C, I'll meet you at the top of the coconut tree." Students can use rhyme to practice the alphabet in *Chicka Chicka Boom Boom* by Bill Martin and John Archambault (Simon & Schuster, 1989).

Learning Center Link

Use construction paper to create word cards for the missing words in the poem. Glue a small Velcro strip to the back of each word card. Glue a Velcro strip above each blank space in the poem. Display at the learning center and challenge children to figure out where each word belongs.

On the Ning Nang Nong

by Spike Milligan

On the Ning Nang Nong
Where the Cows go Bong!
And the Monkeys all say Boo!
There's a Nong Nang Ning
Where the trees go Ping!
And the tea pots Jibber Jabber Joo.
On the Nong Ning Nang
All the mice go Clang!
And you just can't catch 'em when they do!
So it's Ning Nang Nong!
Cows go Bong!
Nong Nang Ning!
Trees go Ping!
Nong Ning Nang!
The mice go Clang!
What a noisy place to belong,
Is the Ning Nang Ning Nang Nong! !

Making Music

Students explore different properties of sound by making their own musical instruments.

Materials

For each group:

◎ 8 empty glass bottles

◎ a metal spoon

◎ a small pitcher of water

◎ food coloring (optional)

Teaching the Lesson

1. Begin by asking students to brainstorm a list of musical instruments they know. Discuss the ways in which each instrument makes its sound: Does it have strings? Do you pound on top of it? Blow into it? Explain that musical instruments work because they make the air around them move, or vibrate, when they are played. The vibrations reach our ears, and our brain turns the vibrations into sounds that we hear.

2. Have students line up their bottles in a horizontal row, with a small space in between each bottle.

3. Instruct students to fill the first bottle with a tiny bit of water, then fill each bottle with a little more water than the one before it until all of the bottles contain water.

4. Ask students to gently tap the side of each bottle with the side of the metal spoon. What do they hear? Which bottles make the highest sounds? Which bottles make the lowest sounds? Encourage students to notice that the more water a bottle has, the deeper the sound. Older students may be ready to record predictions and results for this activity in a science journal.

ACTIVITY Extension Make music composition paper by drawing eight bottles on a piece of paper and making copies for students. Let students use the food coloring to turn the water in each bottle a different color. (This will help students remember the correlation between each bottle and the sound it makes.) Have students create musical compositions, then record them by coloring in the bottles on the paper to match the bottles they play.

Literature Connection *Ty's One-man Band* by Mildred Pitts Walter (Macmillan, 1980) is the story of a traveling man who, with a little boy's help, makes music using a comb, spoons, and a washboard. Children can use these music-makers (substitute running a spoon along a grater for the washboard) to add sound effects as you read the story aloud.

Learning Center Link

Stock your learning center with materials for making more music-makers. Here are three easy instruments to make and play.

DRUMS: Students can make simple drums out of just about any hollow round or tube-shaped objects. Empty coffee cans and oatmeal containers work well. For the drum head, cut out a piece of cloth, contact paper, or plastic bubble wrap about two to three inches wider than the top of the drum. Stretch the material tightly over the top, and secure with a rubber band. Children can decorate their drums with colored paper, paints, and crayons. Which drums make louder or fuller sounds? Higher or thinner sounds?

RATTLES: Make simple rattles by filling empty containers (or paper towel tubes; staple the ends) with pebbles, sand, dried beans, and other materials and tightly closing the lids. Challenge students to create different kinds of rattles: a loud rattle, a rattle that sounds like rain, and so on.

RUBBER BAND HARP: Make harps using rectangular metal loaf pans and thick rubber bands. Slide eight rubber bands around the width of a pan, about 1/2 inch apart. Play by plucking each rubber band. Students might notice that each band makes the same sound. Ask: How do you think you could change the sound each rubber band makes? Let students try out some of their ideas.

Talking Hands

Students learn that sound isn't the only way people communicate with one another.

Background Information

There are many forms of sign language in the worldwide deaf community. American Sign Language (ASL) is one. The language consists of hand movements representing thousands of words and phrases in the English language; the alphabet is normally only used to spell out names and special terms.

Materials

◎ sign language reproducible (see page 23)

Teaching the Lesson

1. Begin by explaining that not everyone's ears can turn vibrations into sound. Some people are hearing impaired, or deaf. Explain that people who are deaf have a special way of communicating with one another called *sign language.*

2. Distribute a copy of the sign language reproducible to each student. Lead students through the alphabet by signing the letters together, one at a time.

3. Divide students into pairs. Ask students to spell out their own names, in sign language, to one another.

4. Wrap up by asking: What sense are you using when you communicate with sign language? (sight) What senses might a person who can't see use to communicate? (hearing, touch)

Let students continue communicating other messages with sign language. Invite students to choose something different each day to sign. For example, instead of saying "Please" one day, students can sign it.

Yes

Please

Thank You

Literature Connection

The Handmade Alphabet by Laura Rankin (Dial, 1991) features photographs that show a hand signing each letter of the alphabet, accompanied by a picture clue. Go further by finding out how real-life kids communicate, learn, and play at a school for the deaf in *Handtalk School* by Mary Beth Mill and George Ancona (Macmillan, 1991).

Learning Center Link

Post the sign-language chart in your Five Senses Learning Center. Near the chart, set up a box of word cards containing simple three- and four-letter words. Invite students to visit the box, pull out a word, and spell it out using sign language.

American Sign Language Symbols

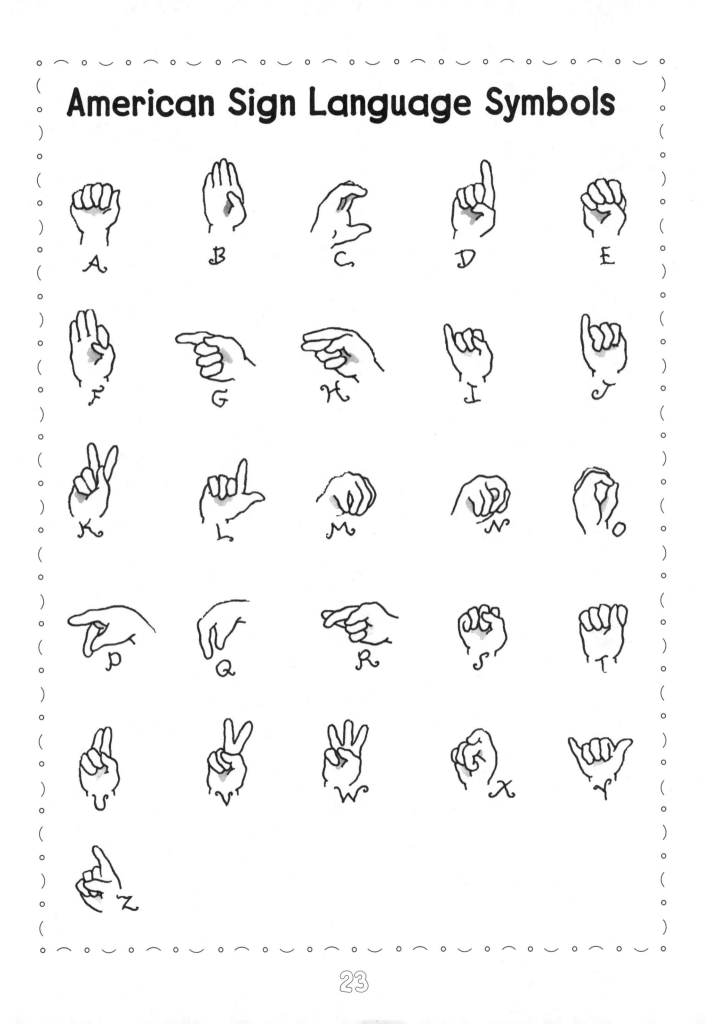

Taste and Smell

Do you know the feeling of your mouth watering at the scent of cookies baking in an oven? This simple phenomenon shows us how closely our senses of taste and smell are linked. In this section we'll explore this connection, and have fun with each sense through games, poetry, and cooking.

SCIENCE NOTES

The tongue is covered with tiny taste buds that pick out the different tastes of food and drink. The nose is packed with tiny hairs and nerves. The hairs trap smells inside the nostrils, and the nerves send messages about the smells to the brain, which interprets them for you. When we eat and drink, these senses work together to form a complete picture of what foods taste like.

Taste Test

Students learn firsthand how taste and smell work together when they perform this fun activity. You'll want students to pair off for this lesson.

Materials

For each pair of students:

- 1 bandanna or strip of cloth to be used as a blindfold (optional)
- 4 carrot sticks
- 4 apple slices
- 4 grapes
- 4 crackers
- record sheet reproducible (see page 31)

Note: *Most foods work well for this activity. Feel free to substitute others for the ones listed here. Before beginning this lesson, check to see if any of your students have allergies to the foods you'll be using. Have students wash their hands.*

Teaching the Lesson

1. Divide students into pairs. Assign each student in a pair the role of tester or taster. (Students will be switching roles.)

2. Instruct the taster in each pair to slip on the blindfold. (Or have students close their eyes.) Have testers record the foods they will be testing on the record sheets.

3. Ask each tester to feed one of the foods to the taster, then ask: Can you tell what food you just ate? Have testers record guesses on the record sheets. Repeat this process with the remaining foods.

4. Repeat steps 2 to 3. This time, ask tasters to hold their noses closed too.

5. Ask students to look at their guesses. Did the tasters have an easier time guessing when they could smell what they were tasting, or when their noses were closed? Encourage students to recognize that their sense of smell works together with their sense of taste. When they can't smell, it's harder to tell what foods taste like.

6. Have testers and tasters switch places and repeat steps 2 to 5.

ACTIVITY Extension To illustrate how accurate and important our sense of smell is, pair up students for another blindfold test. Have children use their noses to guess what a variety of objects are, such as onions, fresh flowers, bubble gum, a lemon, or soap.

Food Favorites

Students use a tasty topic—favorite foods—to gain an appreciation of other

people's opinions and to make a picture graph.

Materials

◎ chart paper

◎ construction paper in a variety of colors

Teaching the Lesson

1 Ask students if they know what a survey is. Explain that people conduct surveys when they want to find out what a group of people think about a subject. Inform students that together, they are going to conduct a survey to find out what the favorite foods of the class are.

2 Survey students, one at a time. Tally responses on the chalkboard. Explain that each tally mark represents one person's answer.

3 Next, turn the results into a picture graph. Use construction paper to cut out shapes that represent the different foods. Set up the graph on chart paper or a bulletin board, as shown below.

4 Invite students to take turns choosing a shape that represents their favorite food, and taping or pasting the shape on the graph. Help students interpret the completed graph by asking questions such as: How many people like pizza best? How do you know that by looking at the graph? Which food do you think is the class favorite? How can you tell?

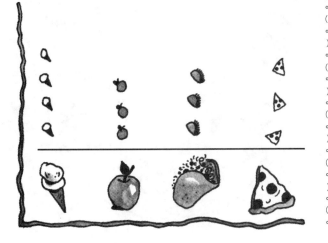

5 Invite students to survey family members and friends about favorite foods. The next day, have students use their results to make their own picture graphs.

Literature Connection Share *Bread, Bread, Bread* by Ann Morris (Morrow, 1993) with students, then take another survey to determine favorite breads (bagels, tortillas, toast, etc.). Have students use the results to make another picture graph.

In *Pot Luck* by Tobi Tobias (Lothrop, 1993), children bring foods that begin with the same letter as each child's name to a potluck celebration. After sharing the story, ask each child to name a food that starts with the first letter of his or her name. Turn responses into a book (Alicia brought apples, Billy brought baked beans, etc.). Let students take turns sharing the potluck story at home.

LANGUAGE ARTS

Three-Step Poems

Working with the favorite foods they've identified in the previous lesson, students create simple three-step poems.

Materials

◎ theme-based stationery (see page 32)

Teaching the Lesson

1 Write the following poem on the chalkboard:

Round and red;
Juicy and sweet;
Apple.

2 Explain how the poem was created. The first line describes how the apple looks.

The second line describes how the apple tastes. The third line states what the apple is.

3 Give each child a piece of theme-based stationery. Ask students to think about what they could write about their favorite foods. You may wish to guide students, one line at a time: Now let's get ready to write the first line of your poem. What does your favorite food look like? Write down words that describe it. Remember, don't tell what it is yet!

4 As students write, encourage them to think about the senses they use to find the words for their poems: The first line of your poems describes how your favorite food looks. What sense do we use to find out how something looks?

5 Display students' poems at the Five Senses Learning Center, or combine them in a Tasty Poems poetry book.

ACTIVITY Extension Use the same three-step process to have students write "Smelly Poems." Here's a model you can use:

> Dirty and messy;
> Very stinky;
> Garbage!

For more theme-based writing, see *Instant Thematic Stationery for Beginning Writers.* (See Professional Resources, page 6.)

Tongue Time

Students practice the skill of classification while learning about the tongue and taste buds.

Materials

◎ 1 sheet of red or pink poster board

◎ construction paper in various colors

◎ marker

◎ hand mirror (optional)

Teaching the Lesson

1 Before you introduce the topic of taste buds, create a tongue poster by cutting a sheet of red or pink poster board in the shape of a tongue. Attach it to a bulletin board or wall space. Using white or light-colored construction paper, write labels for the four types of taste buds: sweet, sour, salty, and bitter. You may wish to add picture clues to each label (an ice cream cone for *sweet*, a lemon for *sour*, a pretzel for *salty*, and a pitcher of iced tea or cup of coffee for *bitter*). Attach the labels to the parts of the tongue where these taste buds are found.

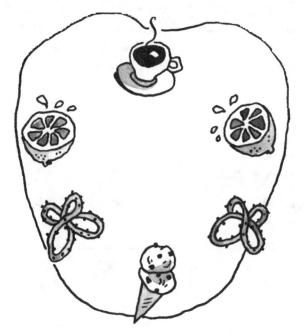

2 When it's time to start the lesson, invite students to look at their own tongues in a mirror, if possible. Can they see the tiny little bumps on their tongues? Explain that these are called taste buds, and that they send messages to our brains about what different foods taste like. Use the tongue poster to help students recognize that different taste buds are located on different parts of the tongue.

3 Ask students to help you finish the tongue poster. Have students draw and cut out pictures of favorite foods. Let students take turns placing their pictures on the poster. As each child tries to match a food with the tongue's taste buds, ask: Where on the tongue do you think you would taste this food? Discuss each choice.

4 When the poster is finished, ask: Where did most of your foods end up? What does this tell you about some of your favorite foods? Which part of the tongue has the least amount of foods near it? Are there any foods that you think could be posted on more than one part of the tongue?

Learning Center Link

Turn the tongue poster into a game. Post the basic tongue poster in the Five Senses Learning Center at a child's height. Glue several Velcro strips to each part of the tongue. Collect pictures of foods and attach a Velcro strip to the back of each. Place the pictures in a box or basket next to the poster. Students can work independently or in small groups to try to put the pictures in the correct places on the tongue.

We Can Cook

Students make a yummy no-cook snack while practicing important skills such as working in groups, measuring, and following directions.

Materials

For each group:

- recipe (see page 33)
- 1-cup dry measuring cup
- mixing bowl
- spoon
- 2 sheets waxed paper
- 1 cup peanut butter
- 1 cup nonfat dry milk
- 1/2 cup raisins
- 1/2 cup flaked coconut

Teaching the Lesson

Note: *Before beginning this lesson, check to find out if students have food allergies to any of the ingredients. Also, you might want to ask older students to help out.*

1 Divide students into groups. Each group will need a clear, clean, flat work space. Students will be handling the food with bare hands, so make sure they're nice and clean!

2 Before diving into the recipe, go over each of the tools and ingredients with students. Can students identify the measuring cup? Do they know how to use the cup to measure out 1/2 cup? Revisit taste buds by inviting students to taste a small bit of the ingredients. Ask: How does this ingredient taste? (Sweet, salty, sour, or bitter?) **Where** would you taste it on your tongue?

3 Give each group a copy of the recipe. As you (or helpers) read aloud each step, have students follow the directions. Interrupt the process periodically to ask questions about the changing textures of the ingredients: What does the peanut butter feel like when you first put it in the mixing bowl? How does the mixture feel after you add the dry milk? Has it changed? If you are conducting this lesson with students who have basic writing skills, select one student in each group to record the process. You may even want to create a record sheet with questions for students to answer as they go along, based on the questions in steps 2 to 4.

4 After cleanup, invite everyone to enjoy their tasty treats. Ask: How do the ingredients taste now that they're all mixed together? What tastes can you identify?

5 Wrap up by discussing changes students noticed when they mixed the ingredients together. Explain that when we combine some substances, a whole new substance forms. Ask students to brainstorm other examples of this principle (instant cocoa and hot water to make hot cocoa; flour, eggs, and milk to make pancakes, and so on).

 Literature Connection These favorite tales feature cooks involved in a step-by-step process:

Jake Baked the Cake by B.G. Hennessy (Viking, 1990)

Thunder Cake by Patricia Pollacco (Philomel, 1990)

Invite students to write or dictate and illustrate their own recipes for making favorite foods. Put students' pages together to make a recipe book. Let students take turns taking it home to share with families.

Taste Test

Tester_____   Taster_____

FOOD	Test 1	Test 2

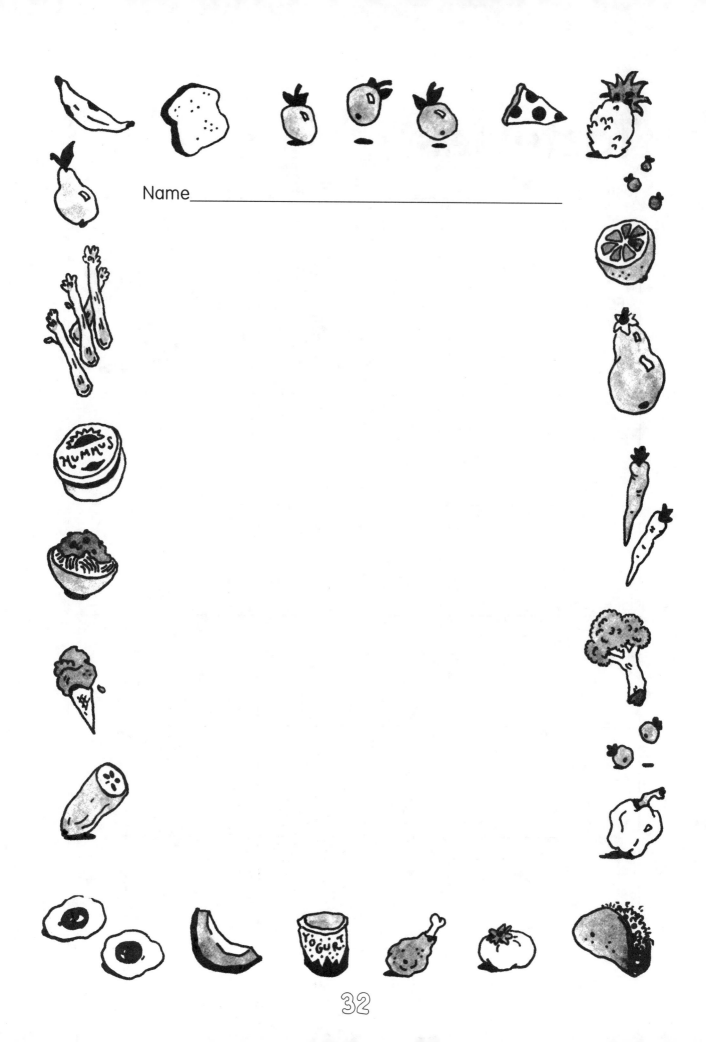

Name_____

Peanut Butter Balls

What You Need

- measuring cup
- peanut butter
- spoon
- dry milk
- bowl
- raisins
- waxed paper
- coconut

What You Do

1. Add 1 [measuring cup] [peanut butter] to the [bowl].

2. Add 1 [measuring cup] [dry milk] to the [bowl].

3. Stir [spoon] the [peanut butter] and the [dry milk] together.

4. Add 1/2 [measuring cup] [raisins] to the [bowl].

5. Stir [spoon] in the [raisins].

6. Use your hands to roll the mixture into little balls.

7. Roll the balls in the [coconut].

8. Put the balls on clean [waxed paper]. Nice job! You're done!

Touch

In this section, the path to learning is literally at your students' fingertips, as they use their sense of touch to explore objects, shapes, and sensations.

SCIENCE NOTES

Hot, cold, smooth, tough, hard, soft... just under the skin are·nerves that send messages to the brain about the way things feel. In some places on the body, such as fingertips, nerves are concentrated, making them more sensitive.

The Guessing Box

Students rely on a single sense—touch—to identify objects hidden from sight.

Materials

For each pair of students:

◎ shoe box (with cover)

◎ 4 or more objects (if possible, choose objects that may be a challenge for children: cooked spaghetti, a seashell, a bar of soap, a bowl of dirt or sand, a string of beads, a lemon, marbles, a leaf, or a pinecone)

◎ two copies of the record sheet reproducible (see page 39)

Teaching the Lesson

1 Prepare for the activity by cutting a hole in the side of each box, wide enough for a child's arm.

2 Divide students into pairs. Assign each student in a pair the role of tester or toucher. (Children will eventually switch roles.)

3 Ask the toucher in each pair to close his or her eyes while the tester selects an object to place inside the box. Have testers record the object (using pictures or words) on the record sheet.

4 Have testers make sure boxes are covered, then ask each toucher to slip his or her hand inside the box and feel the object.

5 Ask the touchers: Can you name the object? Have testers record their guesses on the record sheet (using pictures or words). Repeat this process until touchers have made a guess about all four objects.

6 Instruct students to compare their guesses to actual objects. Ask: How did your sense of touch help you make guesses? How did your sense of touch fool you?

7 Have testers and touchers switch places. Repeat steps 3 to 6. Provide new objects for the second group of touchers to identify.

ACTIVITY Extension Use this activity as a springboard to discuss adjectives—words that describe. On the chalkboard, list all of the objects students tried to identify. Ask students to brainstorm words that describe how each of these things feel. Write the words next to each object, or create a word web of adjectives on chart paper for each object.

Learning Center Link

Place a box of different objects at the center for students to explore on their own. Provide paper so that students can record what they think is inside. After all students have had a chance to visit the mystery box, open it up and let them check their guesses.

Fingerprint Fun

Students investigate their fingertips, the key to their sense of touch, and examine the fingerprints that make each of them unique.

Materials

- reproducible (see page 40)
- ink pad (washable ink)
- blank 3-by-5-inch index cards
- 3 empty shoe boxes
- magnifying glasses (optional)

Teaching the Lesson

1. Ask students to look at their fingertips. Explain that underneath the skin there, thousands of tiny nerves are sending messages to our brains. If children are familiar with what telephone wires do, you can explain that the nerves in their fingertips are like telephone wires—both carry messages. Nerves tell our brains if something is hard or soft, smooth or rough. They also warn us when something is dangerous to touch, such as a sharp object.

2. Next, direct students' attention to the surface of their fingertips. Ask: What do you see? Help students notice the ridges. Ask: Does anyone know what these are called? Point out that no two people in the world have fingerprints that are exactly the same!

3. Give each student an index card. Demonstrate how to make a thumbprint on the card by pressing your thumb on the ink pad, and then onto the card in a firm, even motion. Have each student make a thumbprint, then write his or her name underneath.

4. Hand out the reproducible fingerprint patterns. Explain that even though everyone's fingerprints are different, they all resemble three basic patterns: the arch, the loop, and the whorl. Ask students to compare their fingerprints with the three patterns. Which pattern is most like their own? If possible, let students take a closer look with magnifying glasses so that they can more easily identify their fingerprint patterns.

5. Let students use their cards to make a picture graph. Which pattern is most common in your class?

ACTIVITY Extension Demonstrate how police officers find "invisible" fingerprints. Have students take turns pressing a finger down on a flat, slick surface, such as a metal filing cabinet. Let another student use a paintbrush to brush talcum powder on the surface, then gently blow away the powder to reveal the fingerprint.

READING/LANGUAGE ARTS

Touch a Story

Students make their own mini-books that are fun to touch as well as read.

Materials

- ◎ reproducible mini-book (see pages 41–44)
- ◎ cotton balls, yarn, a container of play sand (available at hardware, plant, and craft stores), buttons, scraps of felt or velour (place these materials in several boxes or baskets at the center)

Teaching the Lesson

Note: *You might want to introduce the lesson by sharing "touchable" books with children, such as* Pat the Beastie *by Henrick Drescher and* The Very Busy Spider *by Eric Carle. Familiarizing children with the type of book they are going to make will help them grasp the concept.*

1. Give each child a set of mini-book pages.

2. Instruct students to cut along the lines on each page, then put the pages together to make a book. Staple along the left side of each child's book, or punch holes and bind with yarn.

3. Read the story together as a class. Then have students look through the boxes of cotton balls and other materials. Ask: What feels like a soft bunny rabbit? What feels like a spiderweb? Invite students to glue materials on the pictures in their books. For example, children might choose cotton balls for the bunny, buttons for the wheels of the car, sand for the beach, felt or velour for the peach, and yarn for the spiderweb.

4. Once again, lead the class in a read-aloud session of the story. This time, students can touch the pictures in their books as they read along.

ACTIVITY Extension Read the story again with students. Ask students to identify words in the story that describe the way things feel (soft, round, rough, smooth, fuzzy, stringy). Write the words on the board. Talk about other words that describe things. Ask students to feel their pencils, desktops, and other items in the classroom. Can they name words that describe how these things feel? Draw a picture of each object on chart paper and record students' words. Display at the center, letting students add new words.

The Guessing Box

Tester_____   Toucher_____

OBJECT IN BOX	MY GUESS

Fingerprint Fun

arch   loop   whorl

Make a fingerprint picture here.

Here's a game that's fun to know.
Use your fingers to touch and go.

Touch and Go

By _____

Touch the round wheels on the car. Go!

Touch the bunny's soft, soft, fur. Go!

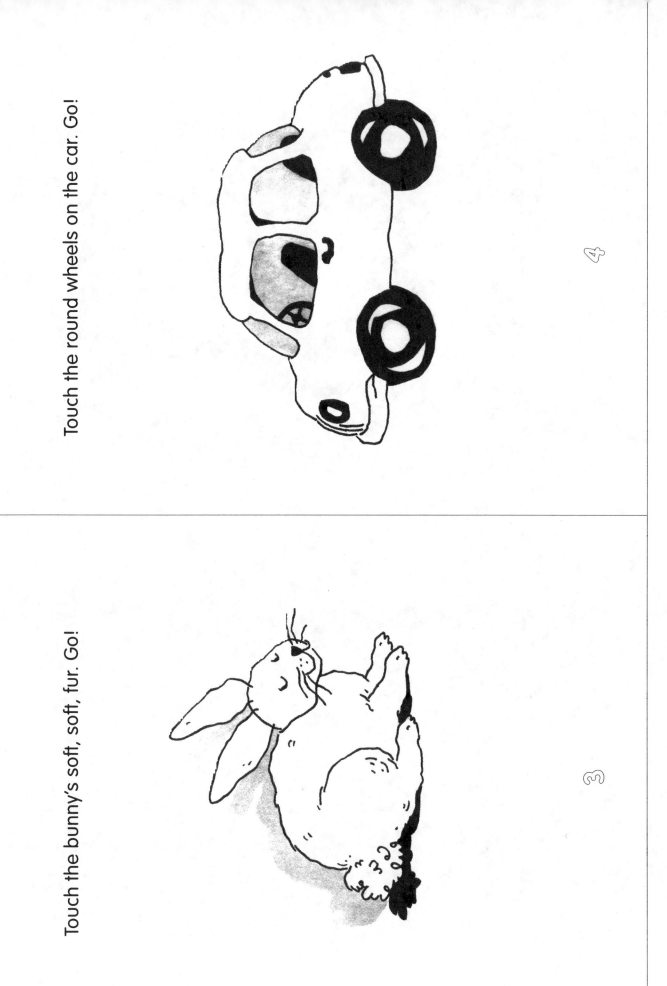

4

3

Touch the smooth and fuzzy peach. Go!

6

Touch the rough and sandy beach. Go!

5

Stop! You're done!
You've reached the end!
Now use this page to make a touch picture
of your own.

Touch the stringy spiderweb. Go!

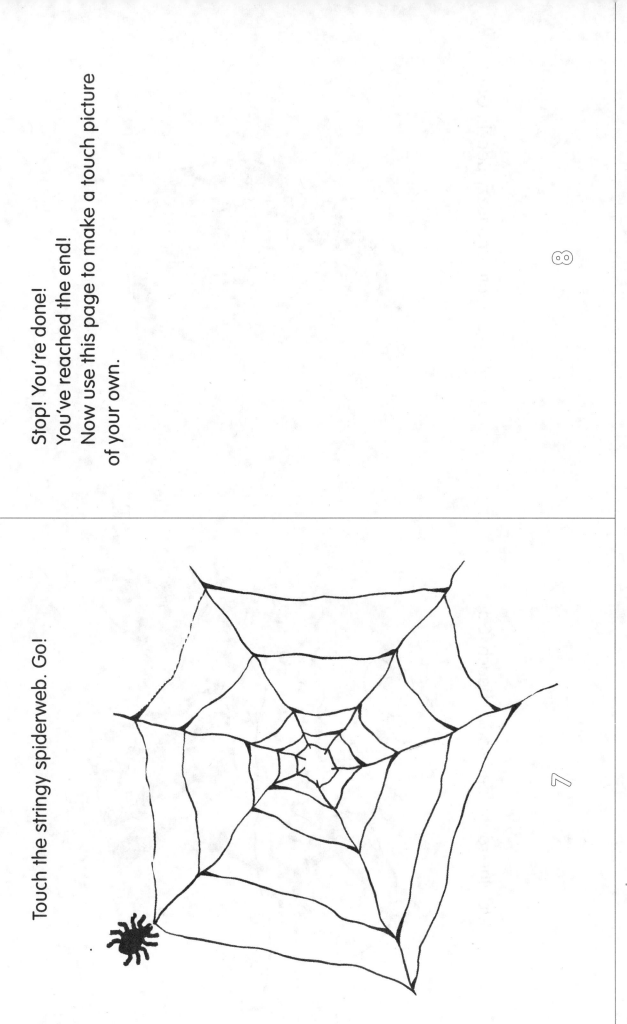

Five Senses Celebration

The activities in this section invite children to review and celebrate what they know about the five senses, while giving you the opportunity to assess their growth.

Sense Webs

Students make word webs that show what they know about the five senses.

Materials

◎ 5 sheets of 11-by-17-inch paper

◎ pencils or crayons

Teaching the Lesson

1 Introduce this activity by creating a word web together on chart paper or a chalkboard. Start with a word that relates to the Five Senses theme, for example, *apple*. Write the word *apple* at the center of the web, then let students suggest words for the spokes of the web that describe how the apple looks and tastes.

2 Divide students into five groups, one for each sense: sight, hearing, touch, taste, smell. If students have been working in groups throughout the unit, you can continue with these groupings.

3 Explain that each group will make its own word web. Have each group start by drawing a picture in the center of a piece of chart paper that represents the group's sense.

4 As you visit with each group, prompt children with questions to help them think of words. For example, ask: What are some things you can smell? Add those words to your web. What are some words that describe how something smells? Add those words, too. Have children do drafts of their webs, first, if you want them to revise invented spelling in a final version.

5 Display webs at the Five Senses Learning Center. If students want to keep going, let them switch senses, so that each group makes a word web for each sense. You can combine webs to make big books, putting each group's pages together to make a book about the five senses or by putting all of the hearing pages together to make a book, all of the sight pages together, and so on.

Literature Connection *Night Sounds, Morning Colors* by Rosemary Wells (Dial Books, 1994) is a beautifully illustrated book about a child who spends a day seeing, hearing, touching, tasting, and smelling the world around him. As you read the story aloud, ask children to identify which sense the child in the story is using on each page.

Find Your Opposite

This interactive game helps students learn and practice the concept of opposites.

Materials

◎ word cards (see below)

◎ safety pins or tape

Teaching the Lesson

1. Make a set of opposite cards using the list below, writing one word on each card. (You'll need one card per student, so add words to the list if necessary.) You may want to add a simple picture to each card to illustrate the word. Place the cards in a bag or basket.

   ◎ hot /cold

   ◎ sweet/sour

   ◎ up/down

   ◎ high/low

   ◎ night/day

   ◎ loud/quiet

   ◎ long/short

   ◎ bumpy/smooth

   ◎ big/small

   ◎ soft/hard

   ◎ round/square

2. Introduce the idea of opposites to students. Begin with a simple example: When the sun is shining on a summer day, how might we feel? (hot) How might we feel on a snowy winter day? (cold) Hot and cold are opposites. Prompt students to think of other words with opposite meanings.

3. Mix up the cards and ask each student to pick a card from the bag. (You'll need an even number of players; you may participate if necessary.) Attach each child's card to the front of his or her shirt with tape or a safety pin.

4. Arrange students in a circle, facing one another. When you say "Go!" each child must try to find his or her partner—the person with the opposite word attached to his or her shirt. Students can hold hands with their partners.

5. After students find their partners, move from pair to pair and read the words aloud. Ask the class: Are these words opposites? If so, children take their seats. If some students are mismatched, see if the class can figure out who really belongs together.

ACTIVITY Extension Let students use the opposite cards to practice classification. What are some ways they can sort the cards? (sight, sound, hearing, taste, and touch) You can prepare envelopes to guide students' sorting, drawing a picture clue on each.

Literature Connection Photograph-to-text correspondence makes *Exactly the Opposite* by Tana Hoban (Greenwillow, 1990) a perfect book for beginning readers. After reading the book, students might be inspired to write their own books about opposites, illustrating with their own drawings or pictures they cut from magazines.

Wrap Up

After your students have spent weeks learning about their five senses, why not wrap up the experience with a special celebration? Designate one day as Five Senses Celebration Day. Invite parents to attend and see what their children have been learning. You can fill the day with some of the activities from previous lessons, and introduce new games and activities as well.

Preparation

Invite children to work in their senses groups to create invitations featuring torn paper pictures that represent each sense. Provide each group with construction paper and tissue paper in assorted colors, as well as paper precut and folded to card size. Ask each group to add a torn-paper picture to each card. The picture should represent the group's sense.

Activities to Share

- ◎ Play games from previous lessons with guests. (See Memory Magic, page 10; The Guessing Box, page 36; Find Your Opposite, page 47.)

- ◎ Play Pin the Tail on the Donkey. Children will learn that getting around isn't easy when we're deprived of our sense of sight.

- ◎ Perform *The City Mouse and the Country Mouse* (see page 17) for parents or play back the tape of your recording session.

- ◎ Invite volunteers in advance to help students whip up another no-cook treat. Encourage children to describe textures, tastes, and smells of different ingredients.

- ◎ Let students use the musical instruments they made (see page 21) to practice and present a musical number for their guests.

- ◎ If students made shadow puppets (see page 13), let them perform a shadow puppet play for guests.

- ◎ Let parents take home their children's Five Senses folders to read and review. Encourage parents to invite their children to tell them about some of the projects in their folders.